Infamous Day

Marines at Pearl Harbor
7 December 1941

Infamous Day

Marines at Pearl Harbor
7 December 1941

Robert J. Cressman
J. Michael Wenger

Vij Books India Pvt Ltd
New Delhi (India)

Published by

Vij Books India Pvt Ltd
(Publishers, Distributors & Importers)
2/19, Ansari Road
Delhi – 110 002
Phones: 91-11-43596460, 91-11-47340674
Mobile: 98110 94883
e-mail: contact@vijpublishing.com
www.vijbooks.in

ISBN: 978-93-93499-41-7

Infamous Day
Marines at Pearl Harbor

On the afternoon of 6 December 1941, Tai Sing Loo, the colorful Pearl Harbor Navy Yard photographer, arranged with Platoon Sergeant Charles R. Christenot, the noncommissioned-officer-in-charge of the Main Gate at the Navy Yard, to have his Marines pose for a photograph between 0830 and 0930 Sunday morning, in front of the new concrete main gate. The photo was to be for a Christmas card.

As war clouds gathered over the Pacific basin in late 1941, the United States Pacific Fleet operated, as it had since May 1940, from Pearl Harbor. While the security of that fleet and for the island of Oahu lay in the Army's hands, that of the Navy Yard and the Naval Air Stations at Pearl Harbor and Kaneohe Bay lay in the hands of Marines. In addition, on board the fleet's battleships, aircraft carriers, and some of its cruisers, Marines provided security, served as orderlies for embarked flag officers and ships' captains, and manned secondary antiaircraft and machine gun batteries—seagoing duties familiar to the Corps since its inception.

The Marine Barracks at Pearl Harbor comprised a Barracks Detachment and two companies, A and B, the men living in a comfortable three-story concrete barracks. Company A manned the main gates at the Submarine Base and Navy Yard, and other "distant outposts," providing yard security, while Company B enforced traffic regulations and maintained proper police and order under the auspices of the Yard Police Officer. In addition, Marines ran the Navy Yard Fire Department. Elements of Marine defense battalions made Pearl Harbor their home, too, residing in the several 100-man temporary wooden barracks buildings that had been completed during 1940 and 1941. Less commodious but no less important was the burgeoning airbase that Marines of Marine Aircraft Group (MAG) 2 (later 21) had hewn and hammered out near Barbers Point—Ewa Mooring Mast Field, home for a Marine aircraft group consisting of fighting, scout-bombing, and utility squadrons.

On 27 November, having been privy to intelligence information gleaned from intercepted and translated Japanese diplomatic message traffic,

Admiral Harold R. Stark, the Chief of Naval Operations, and General George C. Marshall, the Army's Chief of Staff, sent a war warning to their principal commanders on Oahu, Admiral Husband E. Kimmel, the Commander in Chief, Pacific Fleet, and Lieutenant General Walter C. Short, the Commander of the Hawaiian Department. Thus adjured to take appropriate defensive measures, and feeling that his more exposed advance bases needed strengthening, Kimmel set in motion a plan that had been completed as early as 10 November, to provide planes for Midway and Wake. The latter was to receive fighters—12 Grumman F4F-3 Wildcats of Marine Fighter Squadron (VMF) 211—while Midway was to get scout bombers from Marine Scout-Bomber Squadron (VMSB) 231. The following day, 28 November 1941, the carrier *Enterprise* (CV-6) departed Pearl in Task Force 8 under Vice Admiral William F. Halsey, Jr., Commander, Aircraft, Battle Force, embarking VMF-211 at sea. VMSB-231 was to embark in another carrier, *Lexington* (CV-2), in Task Force 12 under Rear Admiral John H. Newton, on 5 December.

National Archives Photo 80-G-451123

Pearl Harbor Navy Yard, looking south, on 13 October 1941. Marine Barracks complex is located to the left of the tank farm visible just to left of center. Several temporary wooden barracks, completed in early 1941, ring the parade ground.

At the outset, apparently no one except the squadron commanders knew their respective destinations, but the men of VMF-211 and VMSB-231, meanwhile, apparently ordered their affairs and made ready for what was to appear as "advanced base exercises." Among those men seeing to his financial affairs at Ewa Mooring Mast Field on 3 December 1941 was First Lieutenant Richard E. Fleming, USMCR, who wrote to his widowed mother: "This is the last time I'll be able to write for probably some time. I'm sorry I can't give you any details; it's that secret."

On the 5th, Task Force 12 sailed from Pearl. Eighteen light gray Vought SB2U-3 Vindicators from VMSB-231, under 41-year old Major Clarence J. "Buddy" Chappell, then made the 1.7-hour flight from Ewa and landed on board *Lexington*, along with the "Lady Lex" air group. Planes recovered, the force set course for Midway. The *Lexington* departed Pearl Harbor on the morning of 5 December. That afternoon saw the arrival of Battleship Division One from gunnery exercises in the Hawaiian Operating Area, and the three dreadnoughts, *Arizona* (BB-39), *Nevada* (BB-36), and *Oklahoma* (BB-37), moored in their assigned berths at the quays along Ford Island. The movements of the ships in and out of Pearl Harbor had been the object of much interest on the part of the espionage system operating out of the Japanese consulate in Honolulu throughout the year 1941, for the information its operatives were providing went to support an ambitious and bold operation that had taken shape over several months.

Unbeknownst to Admiral Kimmel, a Japanese task force under the command of Vice Admiral Chuichi Nagumo, formed around six carriers and the most powerful force of its kind ever assembled by any naval power, had set out from the remote Kurile Islands on 27 November. It observed radio silence and steamed via the comparatively less traveled northern Pacific.

Nagumo's mission was to destroy the United States Pacific Fleet and thus ensure its being unable to threaten the Japanese Southern Operation poised to attack American, British, and Dutch possessions in the Far East. All of the warning signs made available to Admiral Kimmel and General Short pointed toward hostilities occurring within the forseeable future, but not on Oahu. War, however, was about to burst upon the Marines at Pearl Harbor "like a thunderclap from a clear sky."

Suddenly Hurled into War

Some 200 miles north of Oahu, Vice Admiral Nagumo's *First Air Fleet*—formed around the aircraft carriers *Akagi, Kaga, Soryu, Hiryu, Shokaku* and *Zuikaku*—pressed southward in the pre-dawn hours of 7 December 1941. At 0550, the dark gray ships swung to port, into the brisk easterly wind, and commenced launching an initial strike of 184 planes 10 minutes later. A second strike would take off after an hour's interval. Once airborne, the 51 Aichi D3A1 Type 99 dive bombers (Vals), 89 Nakajima B5N2 attack planes (Kates) used in high-level bombing or torpedo bombing roles, and 43 Mitsubishi A6M2 Type 00 fighters (Zeroes), led by Commander Mitsuo Fuchida, *Akagi*'s air group commander, wheeled around, climbed to 3,000 meters, and droned toward the south at 0616. The only other military planes aloft that morning were Douglas SBD Dauntlesses from *Enterprise*, flying searches ahead of the carrier as she returned from Wake Island, Army Boeing B-17 Flying Fortresses heading in from the mainland, and Navy Consolidated PBY Catalinas on routine patrols out of the naval air stations at Ford Island and Kaneohe.

Jordan Collection, MCHC

Aerial view of Ewa Mooring Mast Field, taken 2 December 1941, showing various types of planes arrayed on the mat and living accommodations at middle and right.

That morning, 15 of the ships at Pearl Harbor numbered Marine detachments among their complements: eight battleships, two heavy cruisers, four light cruisers, and one auxiliary. A 16th detachment, assigned to the auxiliary (target/gunnery training ship) *Utah* (AG-16), was ashore on temporary duty at the 14th Naval District Rifle Range at Puuloa Point.

At 0753, Lieutenant Frank Erickson, USCG, the Naval Air Station (NAS) Ford Island duty officer, watched Privates First Class Frank Dudovick and James D. Young, and Private Paul O. Zeller, USMCR—the Marine color guard—march up and take post for Colors. Satisfied that all looked in order outside, Erickson stepped back into the office to check if the assistant officer-of-the-day was ready to play the recording for sounding Colors on the loudspeaker. The sound of two heavy explosions, however, sent the Coast Guard pilot running to the door. He reached it just in time to see a Kate fly past 1010 Dock and release a torpedo. The markings on the plane—"which looked like balls of fire"—left no question as to its identity; the explosion of the torpedo as it struck the battleship *California* (BB-44), moored near the administration building, left no doubt as to its intent.

Jordan Collection, MCHC

The centrally located airship mooring mast at Ewa from which the field derived its distinctive name, February 1941.

National Archives Photo 80-G-32463

While a Marine, foreground, looks skyward, the torpedoed battleship California *(BB-46) lists to port. In the left background flies "Old Glory," raised by PFCs Frank Dudovick and James D. Young, and Pvt Paul O. Zeller, USMCR.*

"The Marines didn't wait for colors," Erickson recalled later, "The flag went right up but the tune was general quarters." As "all Hell" broke loose around them, Dudovick, Young, and Zeller unflinchingly hoisted the Stars and Stripes "with the same smartness and precision" that had characterized their participation in peacetime ceremonies. At the crew barracks on Ford Island, Corporal Clifton Webster and Private First-Class Albert E. Yale headed for the roof immediately after general quarters sounded. In the direct line of fire from strafing planes, they set up a machine gun. Across Oahu, as Japanese planes swept in over NAS Kaneohe Bay, the Marine detachment there—initially the only men who had weapons—hurried to their posts and began firing at the attackers.

Since the American aircraft carriers were at sea, the Japanese targeted the battleships which lay moored off Ford Island. At one end of Battleship Row lay *Nevada*. At 0802, the battleship's .50-caliber machine guns opened fire on the torpedo planes bearing down on them from the direction of the Navy Yard; her gunners believed that they had shot one down almost immediately. An instant later, however, a torpedo penetrated her port side and exploded.

Ahead of *Nevada* lay *Arizona*, with the repair ship *Vestal* (AR-4) alongside, preparing for a tender availability. Major Alan Shapley had been relieved the previous day as detachment commanding officer by Captain John H. Earle, Jr., who had come over to *Arizona* from *Tennessee* (BB-43). Awaiting transportation to the Naval Operating Base, San Diego, and assignment to the 2d Marine Division, Shapley was lingering on board to play first base on the battleship's baseball team in a game scheduled with the squad from the carrier *Enterprise* (CV-6). After the morning meal, he started down to his cabin to change.

Seated at breakfast, Sergeant John M. Baker heard the air raid alarm, followed closely by an explosion in the distance and machine gun fire. Corporal Earl C. Nightingale, leaving the table, had paid no heed to the alarm at the outset, since he had no antiaircraft battle station, but ran to the door on the port side that opened out onto the quarterdeck at the sound of the distant explosion. Looking out, he saw what looked like a bomb splash alongside *Nevada*. Marines from the ship's color guard then burst breathlessly into the messing compartment, saying that they were being attacked.

As general quarters sounded, Baker and Nightingale, among the others, headed for their battle stations. Aft, congestion at the starboard ladder, that led through casemate no. 9, prompted Second Lieutenant Carleton E. Simensen, USMCR, the ship's junior Marine officer, to force his way through. Both Baker and Nightingale noted, in passing, that the 5-inch/51 there was already manned, and Baker heard Corporal Burnis L. Bond, the gun captain, tell the crew to train it out. Nightingale noted that the men seemed "extremely calm and collected."

As Lieutenant Simensen led the Marines up the ladder on the starboard side of the mainmast tripod, an 800-kilogram converted armor-piercing shell dropped by a Kate from *Kaga* ricocheted off the side of Turret IV. Penetrating the deck, it exploded in the vicinity of the captain's pantry. Sergeant Baker was following Simensen up the mainmast when the bomb exploded, shrapnel cutting down the officer as he reached the first platform. He crumpled to the deck. Nightingale, seeing him flat on his back, bent over him to see what he could do but Simensen, dying, motioned for his men to continue on up the ladder. Nightingale continued up to Secondary Aft and reported to Major Shapley that nothing could be done for Simensen.

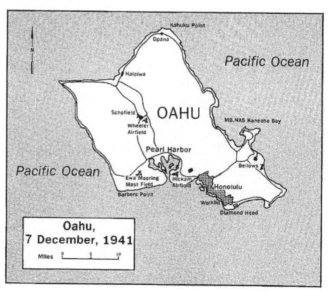

Oahu,
7 December, 1941

An instant later, a rising babble of voices in the secondary station prompted Nightingale to call for silence. No sooner had the tense quiet settled in when, suddenly, a terrible explosion shook the ship, as a second 800-kilogram bomb—dropped by a Kate from *Hiryu*—penetrated the deck near Turret II and set off *Arizona*'s forward magazines. An instant after the terrible fireball mushroomed upward, Nightingale looked out and saw a mass of flames forward of the mainmast, and much in the tradition of Private William Anthony of the *Maine* reported that the ship was afire.A "We'd might as well go below," Major Shapley said, looking around, "we're no good here." Sergeant Baker started down the ladder. Nightingale, the last man out, followed Shapley down the port side of the mast, the railings hot to the touch as they made their way below.

> A Private Anthony, an instant after the explosion mortally damaged the battleship *Maine* in Havana harbor on 15 February 1898, made his way to the captain's cabin, where he encountered that officer in the passageway outside. Drawing himself to attention, Anthony reported that the ship was sinking.

Baker had just reached the searchlight platform when he heard someone shout: "You can't use the ladder." Private First-Class Kenneth D. Goodman, hearing that and apparently assuming (incorrectly, as it turned out) that the ladder down was indeed unusable, instinctively leapt in desperation to the crown of Turret III. Miraculously, he made the jump with only a slight ankle injury. Shapley, Nightingale, and Baker, however, among others, stayed on the ladder and reached the boat deck, only to find it a mass of wreckage and fire, with the bodies of the slain lying thick upon it. Badly charred men staggered to the quarterdeck. Some reached it only to collapse and never rise. Among them was Corporal Bond, burned nearly black, who had been ordering his crew to train out no. 9 5-inch/51 at the outset of the battle; sadly, he would not survive his wounds.

Shapley and Corporal Nightingale made their way across the ship between Turret III and Turret IV, where Shapley stopped to talk with Lieutenant Commander Samuel G. Fuqua, *Arizona*'s first lieutenant and, by that point, the ship's senior officer on board. Fuqua, who appeared "exceptionally calm," as he helped men over the side, listened as Shapley told him that it appeared that a bomb had gone down the stack and triggered the explosion that doomed the ship. Since fighting the massive fires consuming the ship was a hopeless task, Fuqua told the Marine that he had ordered *Arizona* abandoned. Fuqua, the first man Sergeant Baker encountered on the quarterdeck, proved an inspiration. "His calmness gave me courage," Baker later declared, "and I looked around to see if I could help." Fuqua, however, ordered him over the side, too. Baker complied.

Shapley and Nightingale, meanwhile, reached the mooring quay alongside which *Arizona* lay when an explosion blew them into the water. Nightingale started swimming for a pipeline 150 feet away but soon found that his ebbing strength would not permit him to reach it. Shapley, seeing the enlisted man's distress, swam over and grasped his shirt front, and told him to hang onto his shoulders. The strain of swimming with Nightingale, however, proved too much for even the athletic Shapley, who began to experience difficulties himself. Seeing his former detachment commander foundering, Nightingale loosened his grip on his shoulders and told him to go the rest of the way alone. Shapley stopped, however, and firmly grabbed him by the shirt; he refused to let go. "I would have drowned," Nightingale later recounted, "but for the Major." Sergeant Baker had seen their travail, but, too far away to help, made it to Ford Island alone.

Several bombs, meanwhile, fell close aboard *Nevada*, moored astern of *Arizona*, which had begun to hemorrhage fuel from ruptured tanks. Fire spread to the oil that lay thick upon the water, threatening *Nevada*. As the latter counterflooded to correct the list, her acting commanding officer, Lieutenant Commander Francis J. Thomas, USNR, decided that his ship had to get underway "to avoid further danger due to proximity of *Arizona*." After receiving a signal from the yard tower to stand out of the harbor, *Nevada* singled up her lines at 0820. She began moving from her berth 20 minutes later.

Naval Historical Center Photo NH 50931

View from a Japanese plane taken around 0800 on 7 December 1941. At lower left is Nevada *(BB-36), with* Arizona *(BB-39) ahead of her, with the repair ship* Vestal *(AR-4) moored outboard;* West Virginia *(BB-48) (already beginning to list to port) alongside* Tennessee *(BB-43);* Oklahoma *(BB-3) (which has already taken at least one torpedo) with* Maryland *(BB-46) moored inboard; the fleet oiler* Neosho *(AO-23) and, far right,* California *(BB-44), which, too, already has been torpedoed.*

Oklahoma, Nevada's sister ship moored inboard of *Maryland* in berth F-5, meanwhile manned air-defense stations at about 5, to the sound of gunfire. After a junior officer passed the word over the general announcing system that it was not a drill—providing a suffix of profanity to underscore the fact— all men not having an antiaircraft defense station were ordered to lay below the armored deck. Crews at the 5-inch and 3-inch batteries, meanwhile, opened ready-use lockers. A heavy shock, followed by a loud explosion, came soon thereafter as a torpedo slammed home in the battleship's port side. The "Okie" soon began listing to port.

Author's Collection
Col Alan Shapley, in a post-war photograph taken while serving as an aide to Adm William F. Halsey, Jr.

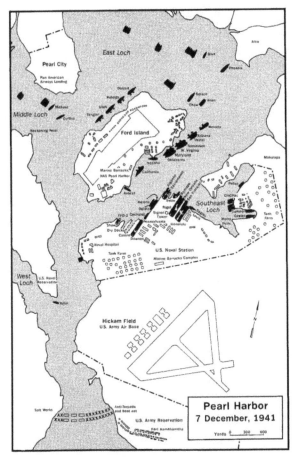

Pearl Harbor

7 December, 1941

Oil and water cascaded over the decks, making them extremely slippery and silencing the ready-duty machine gun on the forward superstructure. Two more torpedoes struck home. The massive rent in the ship's side rendered the desperate attempts at damage control futile. As Ensign Paul H. Backus hurried from his room to his battle station on the signal bridge, he passed his friend Second Lieutenant Harry H. Gaver, Jr., one of *Oklahoma*'s Marine detachment junior officers, "on his knees, attempting to close a hatch on the port side, alongside the barbette [of Turret I] ... part of the trunk which led from the main deck to the magazines.... There were men trying to come up from below at the time Harry was trying to close the hatch...." Backus never saw Gaver again.

As the list increased and the oily, wet decks made even standing up a chore, *Oklahoma*'s acting commanding officer ordered her abandoned to save as many lives as possible. Directed to leave over the starboard side, away from the direction of the roll, most of *Oklahoma*'s men managed to get off, to be picked up by boats arriving to rescue survivors. Sergeant Thomas E. Hailey, and Privates First Class Marlin "S" Seale and James H. Curran, Jr., swam to the nearby *Maryland*. Hailey and Seale turned to the task of rescuing shipmates, Seale remaining on *Maryland*'s blister ledge throughout the attack, pulling men from the water. Later, although inexperienced with that type of weapon, Hailey and Curran manned *Maryland*'s antiaircraft guns. *West Virginia* rescued Privates George B. Bierman and Carl R. McPherson, who not only helped rescue others from the water but also helped to fight that battleship's fires.

National Archives Photo 80-G-32549

Along Battleship Row, beneath a pall of smoke from the burning Arizona (BB-39) *lies* Maryland (BB-46), *her 5-inch/25 antiaircraft battery bristling.* Oklahoma (BB-37) *lies "turned turtle," capsized, at right. This view shows the distance "Okie" survivors swam to the inboard battleship, where they manned antiaircraft batteries and rescued their shipmates.*

Sergeant Woodrow A. Polk, a bomb fragment in his left hip, sprained his right ankle in abandoning ship, while someone clambered into a launch over Sergeant

Leo G. Wears and nearly drowned him in the process. Gunnery Sergeant Norman L. Currier stepped from *Oklahoma*'s red hull to a boat, dry-shod. Wears—as Hailey and Curran—soon found a short-handed antiaircraft gun on *Maryland*'s boat deck and helped pass ammunition. Private First Class Arthur J. Bruktenis, whose column in the December 1941 issue of *The Leatherneck* would be the last to chronicle the peacetime activities of *Oklahoma*'s Marines, dislocated his left shoulder in the abandonment, but survived.

Naval Historical Center Photo NH 102556

Sgt Thomas E. Hailey, 18 May 1942, one month after he had been awarded the Navy Cross for heroism he exhibited on 7 December 1941 that followed the sinking of the battleship Oklahoma *(BB-37).*

Naval Historical Center Photo NH 102557

Cpl Willard A. Darling, circa 1941, was awarded the Navy Cross for heroism in the aftermath of the Japanese air attack on the battleship Oklahoma *(BB-37).*

A little over two weeks shy of his 23d birthday, Corporal Willard D. Darling, an *Oklahoma* Marine who was a native Oklahoman, had meanwhile clambered on board a motor launch. As it headed shoreward, Darling saw 51-year-old Commander Fred M. Rohow (Medical Corps), the capsized battleship's senior medical officer, in a state of shock, struggling in the oily water. Since Rohow seemed to be drowning, Darling unhesitatingly dove in and, along with Shipfitter First Class William S. Thomas, kept him afloat until a second launch picked them up. Strafing Japanese planes and shrapnel from American guns falling around them prompted the abandonment of the launch at a dredge pipeline, so Darling jumped in and directed the doctor to follow him. Again, the Marine rescued Rohow—who proved too exhausted to make it on his own—and towed him to shore.

Maryland, meanwhile, inboard of *Oklahoma*, promptly manned her antiaircraft guns at the outset of the attack, her machine guns opening fire immediately. She took two bomb hits, but suffered only minor damage. Her Marine detachment suffered no casualties.

On board *Tennessee* (BB-43), Marine Captain Chevey S. White, who had just turned 28 the day before, was standing officer-of-the-deck watch as that battleship lay moored inboard of *West Virginia* (BB-48) in berth F-6. Since the commanding officer and the executive officer were both ashore, command devolved upon Lieutenant Commander James W. Adams, Jr., the ship's gunnery officer. Summoned topside at the sound of the general alarm and hearing "all hands to general quarters" over the ship's general announcing system, Adams sprinted to the bridge and spotted White en route. Over the din of battle, Adams shouted for the Marine to "get the ship in condition Zed [Z] as quickly as possible." White did so. By the time Adams reached his battle station on the bridge, White was already at his own battle station, directing the ship's antiaircraft guns. During the action (in which the ship took one bomb that exploded on the center gun of Turret II and another that penetrated the crown of Turret III, the latter breaking apart without exploding), White remained at his unprotected station, coolly and courageously directing the battleship's antiaircraft battery. *Tennessee* claimed four enemy planes shot down.

Marine Corps Historical Collection

Capt Chevey S. White was a veteran of service in China with the 4th Marines, where he had edited the Walla Walla, *the regiment's news magazine. White had become CO of* Tennessee*'s (BB-43) Marine Detachment on 3 August 1941. Ultimately, he was killed by enemy mortar fire on Guam on 22 July 1944.*

West Virginia, outboard of *Tennessee*, had been scheduled to sail for Puget Sound, due for overhaul, on 17 November, but had been retained in Hawaiian waters owing to the tense international situation. In her exposed moorings, she thus absorbed six torpedoes, while a seventh blew her rudder free. Prompt counterflooding, however, prevented her from turning turtle as *Oklahoma* had done, and she sank, upright, alongside *Tennessee*.

On board *California*, moored singly off the administration building at the naval air station, junior officer of the deck on board had been Second Lieutenant Clifford B. Drake. Relieved by Ensign Herbert C. Jones, USNR, Drake went down to the wardroom for breakfast (Kadota figs, followed by steak and eggs) where, around 0755, he heard airplane engines and explosions as Japanese dive bombers attacked the air station. The general quarters alarm then summoned the crew to battle stations. Drake, forsaking his meal, hurried to the foretop.

By 0803, the two ready machine guns forward of the bridge had opened fire, followed shortly thereafter by guns no. 2 and 4 of the antiaircraft battery. As the gunners depleted the ready-use ammunition, however, two torpedoes struck home in quick succession. *California* began to settle as massive flooding occurred. Meanwhile, fumes from the ruptured fuel tanks—she had been fueled to 95 percent capacity the previous day— drove out the men assigned to the party attempting to bring up ammunition for the guns by hand. A call for men to bring up additional gas masks proved fruitless, as the volunteers, who included Private Arthur E. Senior, could not reach the compartment in which they were stored.

California's losing power because of the torpedo damage soon relegated Lieutenant Drake, in her foretop, to the role of "... a reporter of what was going on ... a somewhat confused young lieutenant suddenly hurled into war." As *California* began listing after the torpedo hits, Drake began pondering his own ship's fate. Comparing his ship's list with that of *Oklahoma*'s, he dismissed *California*'s rolling over, thinking, "who ever heard of a battleship capsizing?" *Oklahoma*, however, did a few moments later.

Meanwhile, at about 0810, in response to a call for a chain of volunteers to pass 5-inch/25 ammunition, Private Senior again stepped forward and soon clambered down to the C-L Division Compartment. There he saw Ensign Jones, Lieutenant Drake's relief earlier that morning, standing at the foot of the ladder on the third deck, directing the ammunition supply. For almost 20 minutes, Senior and his shipmates toiled under Jones' direction until a bomb penetrated the main deck at about 0830 and exploded on the second deck, plunging the compartment into darkness. As acrid smoke filled the compartment, Senior reached for his gas mask, which he had lain on a shell box behind him, and put it on. Hearing someone say: "Mr. Jones has been hit," Senior flashed his flashlight over on the ensign's face and saw that "it was all bloody. His white coat also had blood all over it." Senior and another man then carried Jones as far as the M Division compartment, but the ensign would not let them carry him any further. "Leave me alone," he gasped insistently, "I'm done for. Get out of here before the magazines go off!" Soon thereafter, however, before he could get clear, Senior felt the shock of an explosion from down below and collapsed, unconscious.

Naval Historical Center Photo NH 102552

GySgt Charles E. Douglas, 24 February 1941, later awarded the Navy Cross for heroism on board Nevada *at Pearl Harbor. He had seen service in Nicaragua and in the Legation Guard at Peking, as well as at sea in battleships* Pennsylvania *(BB-38) and* New York *(BB-34).*

Naval Historical Center Photo NH 102554

Cpl Joe R. Driskell, circa 1941, later awarded the Navy Cross for heroism on board Nevada *at Pearl Harbor. Driskell had been in the Civilian Conservation Corps in Wyoming before he had enlisted in the Corps. When general quarters sounded on board* Nevada *(BB-36) on 7 December, he took up his battle station as gun captain of no. 9 5-inch/51 gun, in casemate no. 9, on the starboard side.*

Jones' gallantry—which earned him a posthumous Medal of Honor—impressed Private Howard M. Haynes, who had been confined before the attack, awaiting a bad conduct discharge. After the battle, a contrite Haynes—"a mean character who had shown little or no respect for anything or anyone" before 7 December—approached Lieutenant Drake and said that he [Haynes] was alive because of the actions that Ensign Jones had taken. "God," he said, "give me a chance to prove I'm worth it." His actions that morning in the crucible of war earned Haynes a recommendation for retention in the service. Most of *California*'s Marines, like Haynes, survived the battle. Private First Class Earl D. Wallen and Privates Roy E. Lee, Jr. and Shelby C. Shook, however, did not. Nor did the badly burned Private First Class John A. Blount, Jr., who succumbed to his wounds on 9 December.

Nevada's attempt to clear the harbor, meanwhile, inspired those who witnessed it. Her magnificent effort prompted a stepped-up effort by Japanese dive bomber pilots to sink her. One 250-kilogram bomb hit her boat deck just aft of a ventilator trunk and 12 feet to the starboard side of the centerline, about halfway between the stack and the end of the boat deck, setting off laid-out 5-inch ready-use ammunition. Spraying fragments decimated the gun crews. The explosion wrecked the galley and blew open the starboard door of the compartment, venting into casemate no. 9 and starting a fire that swept through the casemate, wrecking the gun. Although he had been seriously wounded by the blast that had hurt both of his legs and stripped much of his uniform from his body, Corporal Joe R. Driskell disregarded his own condition and insisted that he man another gun. He refused medical treatment, assisting other wounded men instead, and then helped battle the flames. He did not quit until those fires were out.

Another 250-kilogram bomb hit *Nevada*'s bridge, penetrating down into casemate no. 6 and starting a fire. The blast had also severed the water pipes providing circulating water to the water-cooled machine guns on the foremast-guns in the charge of Gunnery Sergeant Charles E. Douglas. Intense flames enveloped the forward superstructure, endangering Douglas and his men, and prompting orders for them to abandon their station. They steadfastly remained at their posts, however, keeping the .50-caliber Brownings firing amidst the swirling black smoke until the end of the action.

Unlike the battleships the enemy had caught moored on Battleship Row, *Pennsylvania* (BB-38), the fleet flagship, lay on keel blocks, sharing Dry Dock No. 1 at the Navy Yard with *Cassin* (DD-372) and *Downes* (DD-

375)—two destroyers side-by-side ahead of her. Three of *Pennsylvania*'s four propeller shafts had been removed and she was receiving all steam, power, and water from the yard. Although her being in drydock had excused her from taking part in antiaircraft drills, her crew swiftly manned her machine guns after the first bombs exploded among the PBY flying boats parked on the south end of Ford Island. "Air defense stations" then sounded, followed by "general quarters." Men knocked the locks off ready-use ammunition stowage and *Pennsylvania* opened fire about 0802.

Close-up of the forward superstructure of Nevada (BB 36) taken a few
days after the Japanese
attack as the battleship lay
beached off Waipio Point. In
the upper portion of this view
can be seen the forward
machine gun position with its
four .50-caliber water-cooled
Brownings—the ones manned
by Gunnery Sergeant Douglas
and his men during the battle
on 7 December. Note the extensive fire damage
to the superstruc-
ture below. In the lower
portion of the picture
can be seen one of the
ship's 5-inch/51s, of
the type manned by
Corporal Driskell at
the start of
the action

Close-up of the forward superstructure of Nevada *(BB-36) taken a few days after the Japanese attack as the battleship lay beached off Waipio Point. In the upper portion of this view can be seen the forward machine gun position with its four .50-caliber water-cooled Brownings—the ones manned by Gunnery Sergeant Douglas and his men during the battle on 7 December. Note the extensive fire damage to the superstructure below. In the lower portion of the picture can be seen one of the ship's 5-inch/51s, of the type manned by Corporal Driskell at the start of the action.*

The fleet flagship and the two destroyers nestled in the drydock ahead of her led a charmed life until dive bombers from *Soryu* and *Hiryu* targeted the drydock area between 0830 and 0915.B One bomb penetrated *Pennsylvania*'s boat deck, just to the rear of 5-inch/25 gun no. 7, and detonated in casemate no. 9. Of *Pennsylvania*'s Marine detachment, two men (Privates Patrick P. Tobin and George H. Wade, Jr.) died outright, 13 fell wounded, and six were listed as missing. Three of the wounded— Corporal Morris E. Nations and Jesse C. Vincent, Jr., and Private First-Class Floyd D. Stewart—died later the same day.

B For what became of the two destroyers, and the Marines decorated for bravery in the battle to try to save them, see page 28–29.

Lieutenant Colonel Daniel Russel Fox, USMC, as the Division Marine Officer on the staff of Rear Admiral Isaac C. Kidd, Commander, Battleship Division One, was the most senior Marine officer to die on board *Arizona* on the morning of 7 December 1941. Fox had enlisted in the Marine Corps in 1916. For heroism in France on 4 October 1918, when he was a member of the 17th Company, Fifth Marines, he was awarded the Navy Cross. He also was decorated with the Army's Distinguished Service Cross and the French Croix de Guerre. Fox was commissioned in 1921 and later served in Nicaragua as well as China.

As the onslaught descended upon the battleships and the air station, Marine detachments hurried to their battle stations on board other ships elsewhere at Pearl. In the Navy Yard lay *Argonne* (AG-31), the flagship of the Base Force, the heavy cruisers *New Orleans* (CA-32) and *San Francisco* (CA-38), and the light cruisers *Honolulu* (CL-48), *St. Louis* (CL-49) and *Helena* (CL-50). To the northeast of Ford Island lay the light cruiser *Phoenix* (CL-43).

Although *Utah* was torpedoed and sunk at her berth early in the attack, her 14 Marines, on temporary duty at the 14th Naval District Rifle Range, found useful employment combatting the enemy. The Fleet Machine Gun School lay on Oahu's south coast, west of the Pearl Harbor entrance channel, at Fort Weaver. The men stationed there, including several Marines on temporary duty from the carrier *Enterprise* and the battleships *California* and *Pennsylvania*, sprang to action at the first sounds of war. Working with the men from the Rifle Range, all hands set up and mounted guns, and broke out and belted ammunition between 0755 and 0810. All those present at the range were issued pistols or rifles from the facility's armory.

Soon after the raid began, Platoon Sergeant Harold G. Edwards set about securing the camp against any incursion the Japanese might attempt from the landward side, and also supervised the emplacement of machine guns along the beach. Lieutenant (j.g.) Roy R. Nelson, the officer in charge of the Rifle Range, remembered the many occasions when Captain Frank M. Reinecke, commanding officer of *Utah*'s Marine detachment and the senior instructor at the Fleet Machine Gun School (and, as his Naval Academy classmates remembered, quite a conversationalist), had maintained that the school's weapons would be a great asset if anybody ever attacked Hawaii. By 0810, Reinecke's gunners stood ready to prove the point and soon engaged the enemy—most likely torpedo planes clearing Pearl Harbor or high-level bombers approaching from the south. Nearby Army units, perhaps alerted by the Marines' fire, opened up soon thereafter. Unfortunately, the eager gunners succeeded in downing one of two SBDs from *Enterprise* that were attempting to reach Hickam Field. An Army crash boat, fortunately, rescued the pilot and his wounded passenger soon thereafter.

On board *Argonne*, meanwhile, alongside 1010 Dock, her Marines manned her starboard 3-inch/23 battery and her machine guns. Commander Fred W. Connor, the ship's commanding officer, later credited Corporal Alfred Schlag with shooting down one Japanese plane as it headed for Battleship Row.

When the attack began, *Helena* lay moored alongside 1010 Dock, the venerable minelayer *Oglala* (CM-3) outboard. A signalman, standing watch on the light cruiser's signal bridge at 0757 identified the planes over Ford Island as Japanese, and the ship went to general quarters. Before she could fire a shot in her own defense, however, one 800-kilogram torpedo barrelled into her starboard side about a minute after the general alarm had begun summoning her men to their battle stations. The explosion vented up from the forward engine room through the hatch and passageways, catching many of the crew running to their stations, and started fires on the third deck. Platoon Sergeant Robert W. Teague, Privates First Class Paul F. Huebner, Jr. and George E. Johnson, and Private Lester A. Morris were all severely burned. Johnson later died.

National Archives Photo 80-G-32854

Beneath a leaden sky on 8 December 1941, Marines at NAS Kaneohe Bay fire a volley over the common grave of 15 officers and men killed during the Japanese raid the previous day. Note sandbagged position atop the sandy rise at right.

To the southeast, New Orleans lay across the pier from her sister ship San Francisco. The former went to general quarters soon after enemy planes had been sighted dive-bombing Ford Island around 0757. At 0805, as several low-flying torpedo planes roared by, bound for Battleship Row, Marine sentries on the fantail opened fire with rifles and .45s. *New Orleans'* men, meanwhile, so swiftly manned the 1.1-

inch/75 quads, and .50-caliber machine guns, under the direction of Captain William R. Collins, the commanding officer of the ship's Marine detachment, that the ship actually managed to shoot at torpedo planes passing her stern. *San Francisco*, however, under major overhaul with neither operative armament nor major caliber ammunition on board, was thus restricted to having her men fire small arms at whatever Japanese planes came within range. Some of her crew, though, hurried over to *New Orleans*, which was near-missed by one bomb, and helped man her 5-inchers.

St. Louis, outboard of *Honolulu*, went to general quarters at 0757 and opened fire with her 1.1 quadruple mounted antiaircraft and .50-caliber machine gun batteries, and after getting her 5-inch mounts in commission by 0830—although without power in train—she hauled in her lines at 0847 and got underway at 0931. With all 5-inchers in full commission by 0947, she proceeded to sea, passing the channel entrance buoys abeam around 1000. *Honolulu*, damaged by a near miss from a bomb, remained moored at her berth throughout the action.

Phoenix, moored by herself in berth C-6 in Pearl Harbor, to the northeast of Ford Island, noted the attacking planes at 0755 and went to general quarters. Her machine gun battery opened fire at 0810 on the attacking planes as they came within range; her antiaircraft battery five minutes later. Ultimately, after two false starts (where she had gotten underway and left her berth only to see sortie signals cancelled each time) *Phoenix* cleared the harbor later that day and put to sea.

For at least one Marine, though, the day's adventure was not over when the Japanese planes departed. Search flights took off from Ford Island, pilots taking up utility aircraft with scratch crews, to look for the enemy carriers which had launched the raid. Mustered at the naval air station on Ford Island, *Oklahoma*'s Sergeant Hailey, still clad in his oil-soaked underwear, volunteered to go up in a plane that was leaving on a search mission at around 1130. He remained aloft in the plane, armed with a rifle, for some five hours.

After the attacking planes had retired, the grim business of cleaning up and getting on with the war had to be undertaken. Muster had to be taken to determine who was missing, who was wounded, who lay dead. Men sought out their friends and shipmates. First Lieutenant Cornelius C. Smith, Jr., from the Marine Barracks at the Navy Yard, searched in vain among the maimed and dying at the Naval Hospital later that day, for his friend Harry Gaver from *Oklahoma*. Death respected no rank. The most senior Marine to die that day was Lieutenant Colonel Daniel R. Fox, the decorated World War I hero and the division Marine officer on the staff of the Commander, Battleship Division One, Rear Admiral Isaac C. Kidd, who, along with Lieutenant Colonel Fox, had been killed in *Arizona*. The tragedy of Pearl Harbor struck some families with more force than others: numbered among *Arizona*'s lost were Private Gordon E. Shive, of the battleship's Marine detachment, and his brother, Radioman Third Class Malcolm H. Shive, a member of the ship's company.

Over the next few days, Marines from the sunken ships received reassignment to other vessels—*Nevada*'s Marines deployed ashore to set up defensive positions in the fields adjacent to the grounded and listing battleship—and the dead, those who could be found, were interred with appropriate ceremony. Eventually, the deeds of Marines in the battleship detachments were recognized by appropriate commendations and advancements in ratings. Chief among them, Gunnery Sergeant Douglas, Sergeant Hailey, and Corporals Driskell and Darling were each awarded the Navy Cross. For his "meritorious conduct at the peril of his own life," Major Shapley was commended and awarded the Silver Star. Lieutenant Simensen was awarded a posthumous Bronze Star, while *Tennessee*'s commanding officer commended Captain White for the way in which he had directed that battleship's antiaircraft guns that morning.

Titanic salvage efforts raised some of the sunken battleships—*California*, *West Virginia*, and *Nevada*—and they, like the surviving Marines, went on to play a part in the ultimate defeat of the enemy who had begun the war with such swift and terrible suddenness.

They Caught Us Flat-Footed

At 0740, when Fuchida's fliers had closed to within a few miles of Kahuku Point, the 43 Zeroes split away from the rest of the formation, swinging out north and west of Wheeler Field, the headquarters of the Hawaiian Air Force's 18th Pursuit Wing. Passing further to the south, at about 0745 the *Soryu* and *Hiryu* divisions executed a hard diving turn to port and headed north, toward Wheeler. Eleven Zeroes from *Shokaku* and *Zuikaku* simultaneously left the formation and flew east, crossing over Oahu north of Pearl Harbor to attack NAS Kaneohe Bay. Eighteen from *Akagi* and *Kaga* headed toward what the Japanese called *Babasu Pointo Hikojo* (Barbers Point Airdrome)—Ewa Mooring Mast Field.

Sweeping over the Waianae Range, Lieutenant Commander Shigeru Itaya led *Akagi*'s nine Zeroes, while Lieutenant Yoshio Shiga headed another division of nine from *Kaga*. After the initial attack, Itaya and Shiga were to be followed by divisions from *Soryu*, under Lieutenant Masaji Suganami, and *Hiryu*, under Lieutenant Kiyokuma Okajima, which were, at that moment, involved in attacking Wheeler to the north.

Author's Collection

Ewa Mooring Mast Field, later a Japanese target, is seen hazily through the windshield of a Battleship Row-bound Kate shortly before 0800 on 7 December 1941.

In the officers' mess at Ewa, the officer-of-the-day, Captain Leonard W. Ashwell of VMJ-252, noticed two formations of aircraft at 0755. The first looked like 18 "torpedo planes" flying at 1,000 feet toward Pearl Harbor from Barbers Point, but the second, to the northwest, comprised about 21 planes, just coming over the hills from the direction of Nanakuli, also at an altitude of about 1,000 feet. Ashwell, intrigued by the sight, stepped outside for a better look. The second formation, of single-seat fighters (the two divisions from *Akagi* and *Kaga*), flew just to the north of Ewa and wheeled to the right. Then, flying in a "string" formation, they commenced firing. Recognizing the planes as Japanese, Ashwell burst back into the mess, shouting: "Air Raid ... Air Raid! Pass the word!" He then sprinted for the guard house, to have "call to arms" sounded.

Browning Machine Gun Drill On Board Ship

Marines man a water-cooled, .50-caliber Browning M2 machine gun during a drill on board the gunnery training ship *Wyoming* (AG-17) in late 1941. The M2 Browning weighed (without water) 100 pounds, 8 ounces, and measured five feet, six inches in length. It fired between 550 and 700 rounds per minute to a maximum horizontal range of 7,400 yards. The two hoses carry coolant water to the gun barrel. The gun could be fired without the prescribed two and a half gallons of cooling water—as Gunnery Sergeant Douglas's men did on board *Nevada* (BB-36) on 7 December 1941—but accuracy diminished as the barrel heated and the pattern of shots became more widely dispersed. Experience would reveal that a large number of .50-caliber hits were necessary to disable a plane, and that only a small number of hits could be attained by any single ship-mounted gun against a dive bomber.

That Sunday morning, Technical Sergeant Henry H. Anglin, the noncommissioned-officer-in-charge of the photographic section at Ewa, had driven from his Pearl City home with his three-year-old son, Hank, to take the boy's picture at the station. The senior Anglin had just positioned the lad in front of the camera and was about to take the photo—the picture was to be a gift to the boy's grandparents—when they heard the "mingled noise of airplanes and machine guns." Roaring down to within 25 feet of the ground, Itaya's group most likely carried out only one pass at their targets before moving on to Hickam, the headquarters of the Hawaiian Air Forces 18th Bombardment Wing.

Prange

LCdr Shigeru Itaya, commander of Akagi's *first-wave fighters, which carried out the initial strafing attacks at Ewa Field.*

Thinking that Army pilots were showing off, Sergeant Anglin stepped outside the photographic section tent and, along with some other enlisted men, watched planes bearing Japanese markings strafing the edge of the field. Then, the planes began roaring down toward the field itself and the bullets from their cowl and wing-mounted guns began kicking up puffs of dirt. "Look, live ammunition," somebody said or thought, "Somebody'll go to prison for this."

Shiga's pilots, like Itaya's, concentrated on the tactical aircraft lined up neatly on Ewa's northwest apron with short bursts of 7.7- and 20-millimeter machine gun fire. Shiga's pilots, unlike Itaya's, however, reversed course over the treetops and repeated their blistering attacks from the opposite direction. Within minutes, most of MAG-21's planes sat ablaze and exploding, black smoke corkscrewing into the sky. The enemy spared none of the planes: the gray SBD-1s and -2s of VMSB-232 and the seven spare SB2U-3s left behind by VMSB-231 when they embarked in *Lexington* just two days before. VMF-211's remaining F4F-3s, left behind when the squadron deployed to Wake well over a week before, likewise began exploding in flame and smoke.

At his home on Ewa Beach, three miles southeast of the air station, Captain Richard C. Mangrum, VMSB-232's flight officer, sat reading the Sunday comics. Often residents of that area had heard gunnery exercises, but on a Sunday morning? The chatter of gunfire and the dull thump of explosions, however, drew Mangrum's attention away from the cartoons. As he looked out his front door, planes with red ball markings on the wings and fuselage roared by at very low altitude, bound for Pearl Harbor. Up the valley in the direction of Wheeler Field, smoke was boiling skyward, as it was from Ewa. As he set out for Ewa on an old country road, wives and children of Marines who lived in the Ewa Beach neighborhood began gathering at the Mangrum's house.

Author's Collection

A Mitsubishi A6M2 Zero, flown by PO2 Masao Taniguchi in the 7 December attack on Ewa Mooring Mast Field, takes off from the carrier Akagi, *circa spring 1942.*

Prange

Lt Yoshio Shiga, commander of Kaga's nine Zeroes which strafed Ewa soon after Itaya, was assigned the task of reducing the "Barbers Point Airdrome."

Elsewhere in the Ewa Beach community, Mrs. Charles S. Barker, Jr., wife of Master Technical Sergeant Barker, the chief clerk in MAG-21's operations office, heard the noise and asked: "What's all the shooting?" Barker, clad only in beach shorts, looked out his front door, saw and heard a plane fly by at low altitude, and then saw splashes along the shoreline from strafing planes marked with red *hinomaru*. Running out to turn off the water hose in his front yard, and seeing a small explosion nearby (probably an antiaircraft shell from the direction of Pearl), Barker had seen enough. He left his wife and baby with his neighbors, and set out for Ewa.

The strafers who singled out cars moving along the roads that led to Ewa proved no respecter of persons. MAG-21's commanding officer, Lieutenant Colonel Claude A. "Sheriff" Larkin, en route from Honolulu, was about a mile from Ewa in his 1930 Plymouth when a Zero shot at him. He momentarily abandoned the car for the relative sanctuary of a nearby ditch, not even bothering to turn off the engine, and then, as the strafer roared out of sight, sprinted back to the vehicle, jumped back in, and sped on. He reached his destination at 0805—just in time to be machine gunned again by one of Admiral Nagumo's fighters. Soon thereafter, Larkin's good fortune at remaining unwounded amidst the attack ran out, as he suffered several penetrating wounds, the most painful of which included one on the top of the middle finger of his left hand and another on the front of his lower left leg just above the top of his shoe. Refusing immediate medical attention, though, Larkin continued to direct the defense of Ewa Field.

Jordan Collection, MCHC

TSgt Henry H. Anglin, the noncommissioned officer in charge of Ewa's Photography Section, stands before the mooring mast field's dispensary on 8 December 1941, solemnly displaying the slug that wounded him on the 7th.

Pilots and ground crewmen alike rushed out onto the mat to try to save their planes from certain destruction. At least a few pilots intended to get airborne, but could not because most of their aircraft were either afire or riddled beyond any hope of immediate use.

Captain Milo G. Haines of VMF-211 sought safety behind a tractor, he and the machine's driver taking shelter on the side opposite to the strafers. Another Zero came in from another angle, however, and strafed them from that direction. Spraying bullets clipped off Haines' necktie just beneath his chin. Then, as a momentarily relieved Haines put his right hand at the back of his head a bullet lacerated his right little finger and a part of his scalp.

In the midst of the confusion, an excited three-year-old Hank Anglin innocently took advantage of his father's distraction with the battle and wandered toward the mat. All of the noise seemed like a lot of fun. Sergeant Anglin ran after his son, got him to the ground, and, shielding him with his own body, crawled some 35 yards, little puffs of dirt coming near them at times. As they clambered inside the radio trailer to get out of harm's way, a bullet made a hole above the door. Moving back to the photo tent, the elder Anglin put his son under a wooden bench. As he set about gathering his camera gear to take pictures of the action, a bullet went through his left arm. Deprived of the use of that arm for a time, Anglin returned to the bench under which his son still crouched obediently, to see little Hank point to a spent bullet on the floor and hear him warn: "Don't touch that, daddy, it's hot."

Larkin Collection, MCHC

One of the seven Vought SB2U-3s destroyed on the field at Ewa. All of VMSB-231's spares (the squadron was embarked in Lexington, *en route to Midway, at the time) were thus destroyed. In the background is one of VMSB-232's SBDs.*

Private First Class James W. Mann, the driver assigned to Ewa's 1938 Ford ambulance, had been refueling the vehicle when the attack began. When Lieutenant Thomas L. Allman, Medical Corps, USN, the group medical officer, saw the first planes break into flames, he ordered Mann to take the ambulance to the flight line. Accompanied by Pharmacist's Mate 2d Class Orin D. Smith, a corpsman from sick bay, they sped off. The Japanese planes seemed to be attracted to the bright red crosses on the ambulance, however, and halted its progress near the mooring mast. Realizing that they were under attack, Mann floored the brake pedal and the Ford screeched to a halt. Rather than leave the vehicle for a safer area, Mann and Smith crawled underneath it so that they could continue their mission as quickly as possible. The strafing, however, continued unabated. Ironically, the first casualty Mann had to collect was the man lying prone beside him. Orin Smith felt a searing pain as one of the Japanese 7.7-millimeter rounds found its mark in the fleshy part of his left calf. Seeing that the corpsman had been hurt, Mann assisted him out from under the vehicle and up into the cab. Despite continued strafing that shot out four tires, Mann pressed doggedly ahead and delivered the wounded Smith to sick bay.

Larkin Collection, MCHC

Col Claude A. "Sheriff" Larkin, Commanding Officer, Marine Aircraft Group 21, photographed circa early 1942.

After seeing that the corpsman's bleeding was stopped and the painful wound was cleaned and dressed, Private First Class Mann sprinted to his own tent. Grabbing his rifle, he then returned to the battered ambulance and, shot-out tires flopping, drove toward Ewa's garage. There, Master Technical Sergeant Lawrence R. Darner directed his men to replace the damaged tires with those from a mobile water purifier. Meanwhile, Smith resumed his duties as a member of the dressing station crew.

Also watching the smoke beginning to billow skyward was Sergeant Duane W. Shaw, USMCR, the driver of the station fire truck. Normally, during off-duty hours, the truck sat parked a quarter-mile from the landing area. Shaw, figuring that it was his job to put out the fires, climbed into the fire engine and set off. Unfortunately, like Private First Class Mann's ambulance, Sergeant Shaw's bright red engine moving across the embattled camp soon attracted strafing Zeroes. Unfazed by the enemy fire that perforated his vehicle in several places, he drove doggedly toward the flight line until another Zero shot out his tires. Only then pausing to make a hasty estimate of the situation, he reasoned that with the fire truck at least temporarily out of service he would have to do something else. Jumping down from the cab, he soon got himself a rifle and some ammunition. Then, he set out for the flight line. If he could not put out fires, he could at least do some firing of his own at the men who caused them.

With the parking area cloaked in black smoke, Japanese fighter pilots shifted their efforts to the planes either out for repairs in the rear areas or to the utility planes parked north of the intersection of the main runways. Inside ten minutes' time, machine gun fire likewise transformed many of those planes into flaming wreckage.

Firing only small arms and rifles in the opening stages, the Marines fought back against *Kaga*'s fighters as best they could, with almost reckless heroism. Lieutenant Shiga remembered one particular Leatherneck who, oblivious to the machine gun fire striking the ground around him and kicking up dirt, stood transfixed, emptying his sidearm at Shiga's Zero as it roared past. Years later, Shiga would describe that lone, defiant, and unknown Marine as the bravest American he had ever met.

A tragic drama, however, soon unfolded amidst the Japanese attack. One Marine, Sergeant William E. Lutschan, Jr., USMCR, a truckdriver, had been "under suspicion" of espionage and he was ordered placed under arrest. In the exchange of gunfire that followed his resisting being taken into custody, though, he was shot dead. With that one exception, the Marines at Ewa Field had fought back to a man.

Larkin Collection, MCHC

Ewa's 1938 Ford ambulance, seen after the Japanese raid, its Red Cross status violated, took over 50 hits from strafing planes.

As if *Akagi*'s and *Kaga*'s fighters had not sown enough destruction on Ewa, one division of Zeroes from *Soryu* and one from *Hiryu* arrived on the scene, fresh from laying waste to many of the planes at Wheeler Field. This second group of fighter pilots went about their work with the same deadly precision exhibited at Wheeler only minutes before. The raid caught Master Technical Sergeant Darner's crew in the middle of changing the tires on the station's ambulance. Private First Class Mann, who by that point had managed to obtain some ammunition for his rifle, dropped down with the rest of the Marines at the garage and fired at the attacking fighters as they streaked by.

Lieutenant Kiyokuma Okajima led his six fighters down through the rolling smoke, executing strafing attacks until ground fire holed the forward fuel tank of his wingman, Petty Officer 1st Class Kazuo

Muranaka. When Okajima discovered the damage to Muranaka's plane, he decided that his men had pressed their luck far enough, and began to assemble his unit and shepherd them toward the rendezvous area some 10 miles west of Kaena Point. The retiring Japanese in all likelihood then spotted incoming planes from *Enterprise* (CV-6), that had been launched at 0618 to scout 150 miles ahead of the ship in nine two-plane sections. Their planned flight path to Pearl was to take many of them over Ewa Mooring Mast Field, where some would encounter Japanese aircraft.

Meanwhile, back at Ewa, after what must have seemed an eternity, the Zeroes of the first wave at last wheeled away toward their rendezvous point. Having made a shambles of the Marine air base, Japanese pilots claimed the destruction of 60 aircraft on the ground: *Akagi*'s airmen accounted for 11, *Kaga*'s 15, *Soryu*'s 12, and *Hiryu*'s 22. Their figures were not too far off the mark, for 47 aircraft of all types had been parked at the field at the beginning of the onslaught, 33 of which had been fully operational.

Although the Japanese had wreaked havoc upon MAG-21's complement of planes, the group's casualties seemed miraculously light. Apparently, the enemy fighter pilots in the first wave maintained a fairly high degree of discipline, eschewing attacks on people and concentrating their attacks on machines. Many of Ewa's Marines, however, had parked their cars near the center of the station. By the time the Japanese departed, the parking lot resembled a junk yard of mangled automobiles of various makes and models.

Overcoming the initial shock of the first strafing attack, Ewa's Marines took stock of their situation. As soon as the last of Itaya's and Shiga's Zeroes had departed, Marines went out and manned stations with rifles and .30-caliber machine guns taken from damaged aircraft and from the squadron ordnance rooms. Technical Sergeant William G. Turnage, an armorer, supervised the setting up of the free machine guns. Technical Sergeant Anglin, meanwhile, took his little boy to the guard house, where a woman motorist agreed to drive Hank home to his mother. As it would turn out, that reunion was not to be accomplished until much later that day, "inasmuch as the distraught mother had already left home to look for her son."

Master Technical Sergeant Emil S. Peters, a veteran of action in Nicaragua, had, during the first attack, reported to the central ordnance tent to lend a hand in manning a gun. By the time he arrived there, however, there were none left to man. Then he saw a Douglas SBD-2, one of two spares assigned to VMSB-232, parked behind the squadron's tents. Enlisting the aid of Private William G. Turner, VMSB-231's squadron clerk, Peters ran over to the ex-*Lexington* machine that still bore her USN markings, 2-B-6, pulled the after canopy forward, and clambered in the after cockpit, stepping hard on the foot pedal to unship the free .30-caliber Browning from its housing in the after fuselage, and then locking it in place. Turner, having obtained a supply of belted ammunition, took his place on the wing as Peters' assistant.

Elsewhere, nursing his painfully wounded finger and leg, Lieutenant Colonel Larkin ordered extra guards posted on the perimeter of the field and on the various roads leading into the base. Men not engaged in active defense went to work fighting the many fires. Drivers parked what trucks and automobiles had remained intact on the runways to prevent any possible landings by airborne troops. Although hardly transforming Ewa into a fortress, the Marines ensured that they would be ready for any future attack.

Undoubtedly, most of the men at Ewa expected—correctly—that the Japanese would return. At about 0835, enemy planes again made their appearance in the sky over Ewa, but this time, Marines stood or crouched ready and waiting for what proved to be Lieutenant Commander Takahashi's dive bombing unit from *Shokaku*, returning from its attacks on the naval air station at Pearl Harbor and the Army's Hickam Field, roaring in from just above the treetops. Initially, their targets appeared to be the planes, but, seeing that most had already been destroyed, the enemy pilots turned to strafing buildings and people in a "heavy and prolonged" assault.

Lord Collection, USMC

At their barracks, near the foundation of a swimming pool under construction, three Marines gingerly seek out good vantage points from which to fire, while two peer skyward, keeping their eyes peeled for attacking Japanese planes.

Headgear varies from Hawley helmet to garrison cap to none, but the weapon is the same for all—the Springfield 1903 rifle.

Better prepared than they had been when Lieutenant Commander Itaya's Zeroes had opened the battle, Ewa's Marines met Takahashi's Vals with heavy fire from rifles, Thompson submachine guns, .30-caliber machine guns, and even pistols. In retaliation, after completing their strafing runs, the Japanese pilots pulled up in steep wing-overs, allowing their rear seat gunners to take advantage of the favorable deflection angle to spray the defenders with 7.7-millimeter bullets. Marine observers later recounted that *Shokaku*'s planes also dropped light bombs, perhaps of the 60-kilogram variety, as they counted five small craters on the field after the attack.

In response to the second onslaught, as they had in the first, all available Marines threw themselves into the desperate defense of their base. The additional strafing attacks started numerous fires within the camp area, adding new columns of dense smoke to those still rising from the planes on the parking apron. Unfortunately, the ground fire seemed far more brave than accurate, because all of *Shokaku*'s dive bombers repeatedly zoomed skyward, seemingly unhurt. Even taking into account possible damage sustained during attacks over Ford Island and Hickam, only four of Takahashi's planes sustained any damage over Oahu before they retired. The departure of *Shokaku*'s Vals afforded Lieutenant Colonel Larkin the opportunity to reorganize the camp defenses. There was ammunition to be distributed, wounded men to be succored, and seemingly innumerable fires burning amongst the tents, buildings, and planes, to be extinguished.

However, around 0930, yet another flight of enemy planes appeared—about 15 Vals from *Kaga* and *Hiryu*. Although the pilots of those planes had expended their 250-kilogram bombs on ships at Pearl Harbor, they still apparently retained plenty of 7.7-millimeter ammunition, and seemed determined to expend much of what remained upon Ewa. As in the previous attacks by *Shokaku*'s Vals, the last group came in at very low altitude from just over the tops of the trees surrounding the station. Quite taken by the high maneuverability of the nimble dive bombers, which they were seeing at close hand for the second time that day, the Marines mistook them for fighter aircraft with fixed landing gear.

Marine Corps Historical Collection

Sgt William G. Turnage enlisted in the Corps in 1931. Recommended for a letter of commendation for his "efficient action" at Ewa Field on 7 December, he ultimately was awarded a Bronze Star.

Around that time, Lieutenant Colonel Larkin saw an American plane and a Japanese one collide in mid-air a short distance away from the field. In all probability, Larkin saw *Enterprise*'s Ensign John H. L. Vogt's Dauntless collide with a Val. Vogt had become separated from his section leader during the Pearl-bound flight in from the carrier, may have circled offshore, and then arrived over Ewa in time to encounter dive bombers from *Kaga* or *Hiryu*. Vogt and his passenger, Radioman Third Class Sidney Pierce, bailed out of their SBD, but at too low an altitude, for both died in the trees when their 'chutes failed to deploy fully. Neither of the Japanese crewmen escaped from their Val when it crashed.

Naval Historical Center Photo
NH 102278

TSgt Emil S. Peters, seen here on 11 October 1938, was a veteran of service in Nicaragua and a little more than three weeks shy of his 48th birthday when Japanese bombers attacked Ewa Field.

Fortunately for the Marines, however, the last raid proved comparatively "light and ineffectual," something Lieutenant Colonel Larkin attributed to the heavy gunfire thrown skyward. The short respite between the second and third strafing attacks had allowed Ewa's defenders to bring all possible weapons to bear against the Japanese. Technical Sergeant Turnage, after having gotten the base's machine guns set up and ready for action, took over one of the mounts himself and fired several bursts into the belly of one Val that began trailing smoke and began to falter soon thereafter.

Turnage, however, was by no means the only Marine using his weapon to good effect. Master Technical Sergeant Peters and Private Turner, from their improvised position in the lamed SBD, had let fly at whatever Vals came within range of their gun. The two Marines shot down what witnesses thought were at least two of the attacking planes and discouraged strafing in that area of the station. However, the Japanese soon tired of the tenacious bravery of the grizzled veteran and the young clerk, neither of whom flinched in the face of repeated strafing. Two particular enemy pilots repeatedly peppered the grounded Dauntless with 7.7-millimeter fire, ultimately scoring hits near the cockpit area and wounding both men. Turner toppled from the wing, mortally wounded.

Another Marine who distinguished himself during the third strafing attack was Sergeant Carlo A. Micheletto of Marine Utility Squadron (VMJ) 252. During the first Japanese attack that morning, Micheletto proceeded at once to VMJ-252's parking area and went to work, helping in the attempts to extinguish the fires that had broken out amongst the squadron's parked utility planes. He continued in those labors until the last strafing attack began. Putting aside his firefighting equipment and grabbing a rifle, he took cover behind a small pile of lumber, and heedless of the heavy machine-gunning, continued to fire at the attacking planes until a burst of enemy fire struck him in the head and killed him instantly.

Eventually, in an almost predictable way, the Japanese planes formed up and flew off to the west, leaving the once neatly manicured Mooring Mast Field smouldering. The Marines had barely had time to catch their collective breath when, at 1000, almost as a capstone to the complete chaos wreaked by the initial Japanese attack, seven more planes arrived.

*   *   *   *   *

Their markings, however, were of a more familiar variety—red-centered blue and white stars. The newcomers proved to be a group of Dauntlesses from *Enterprise*. For the better part of an hour, Lieutenant Wilmer E. Gallaher, executive officer of Scouting Squadron 6, had circled fitfully over the Pacific swells south of Oahu, waiting for the situation there to settle down. At about 0945, when he had seen that the skies seemed relatively clear of Japanese planes, Gallaher decided rather than face friendly fire over Pearl he would go to Ewa instead. They had barely stopped on the strip, however, when a Marine ran out to Gallaher's plane and yelled, "For God's sake, get into the air or they'll strafe you, too!" Other *Enterprise* pilots likewise saw ground crews frantically motioning for them to take off immediately. Instructed to "take off and stay in the air until [the] air raid was over," the *Enterprise* pilots took off and headed for Pearl Harbor. Although all seven SBDs left Ewa, only three (Gallaher's, his wingman, Ensign William P. West's, and Ensign Cleo J. Dobson's) would make it as far as Ford Island. A tremendous volume of antiaircraft fire over the harbor rose to meet what was thought to be yet another attack; seeing the reception accorded Gallaher, West, and Dobson, the other four pilots—Lieutenant (jg) Hart D. Hilton and Ensigns Carlton T. Fogg, Edwin J. Kroeger, and Frederick T. Weber— wheeled around and headed back to Ewa, landing around 1015 to find a far better reception that time around. Within a matter of minutes, the Marines began rearming and refueling Hilton's, Kroeger's and Weber's SBDs. The Marines discovered that Fogg's Dauntless, though, had taken a hit that had holed a fuel tank, and would require repairs.

Although it is unlikely that even one of the Ewa Marines thought so at the time, even as they serviced the *Enterprise* SBDs which sat on the landing mat, the Japanese raid on Oahu was over. Vice Admiral Nagumo, already feeling that he had pushed his luck far enough, was eager to get as far away from the waters north of Oahu as soon as possible. At least for the time being, the Marines at Ewa had nothing to fear.

Marine Corps Historical Collection

Sgt Carlo A. Micheletto had turned 26 years old less than two months before Japanese planes strafed Ewa. He was recommended for a letter of commendation, but was awarded a Bronze Star.

Not privy to the musings of Nagumo and his staff, however, Lieutenant Colonel Larkin could only wonder what the Marines would do should the Japanese return. At 1025, he completed a glum assessment of the situation and forwarded it to Admiral Kimmel. While casualties among the Marines had been light—two men had been killed and several wounded—the Japanese had destroyed "all bombing, fighting, and transport planes" on the ground. Ewa had no radio communications, no power, and only one small gas generator in commission. He also informed the Commander-in-Chief, Pacific Fleet, that he would retain the four Enterprise planes at Ewa until further orders. Larkin also notified Wheeler Field Control of the SBDs being held at his field.

At 1100, Wheeler called and directed all available planes to rendezvous with a flight of B-17s over Hickam. Lieutenant (jg) Hilton and the two ensigns from Bombing Squadron 6, Kroeger and Weber, took off at 1115 and the Marines never heard from them again. Finding no Army planes over Hickam (two flights of B-17s and Douglas A-20s had only just departed) the three Navy pilots landed at Ford Island. Ensign Fogg's SBD represented the sole naval strike capability at Ewa as the day ended.

"They caught us flat-footed," Larkin unabashedly wrote Major General Ross E. Rowell of the events of 7 December. Over the next few months, Ewa would serve as the focal point for Marine aviation activities on Oahu as the service acquired replacement aircraft and began rebuilding to carry out the mission of standing ready to deploy with the fleet wherever it was required.

They're Kicking the Hell Out of Pearl Harbor

Although the Japanese accorded the battleships and air facilities priority as targets for destruction on the morning of 7 December 1941, it was natural that the onslaught touched the Marine Barracks at Pearl Harbor Navy Yard as well.

Colonel William E. Farthing, Army Air Forces, commanding officer of Hickam Field, thought that he was witnessing some very realistic maneuvers shortly before 0800 that morning. From his vantage point, virtually next door to the Navy Yard, Farthing watched what proved to be six Japanese dive bombers swooping down toward Ford Island. He thought that MAG-21's SB2Us or SBDs were out for an early morning practice hop. "I wonder what the Marines are doing to the Navy so early Sunday?"

Over at the Marine Barracks, the officer of the guard, Second Lieutenant Arnold D. Swartz, after having inspected his sentries, had retired to the officer-of-the-day's room to await breakfast. Stepping out onto the lanai (patio) at about 0755 to talk to the field music about morning colors, he noticed several planes diving in the direction of the naval air station. He thought initially that it seemed a bit early for practice bombing, but then saw a flash and heard the resulting explosion that immediately dispelled any illusions he might have held that what he was seeing was merely an exercise. Seeing a plane with "red balls" on the wings roar by at low level convinced Swartz that Japanese planes were attacking.

Major Harold C. Roberts had earned a Navy Cross as a corpsman assigned to Marines during World War I, and a second award in 1928 as a Marine officer in Nicaragua. As acting commanding officer of the 3d Defense Battalion at Pearl Harbor on 7 December, he was a veritable dynamo, organizing it to battle the attacking Japanese. He was killed at Okinawa in June 1945 while commanding the 22d Marines, but not before his performance of duty had merited him the award of his third Navy Cross.

Over in the squad room of Barracks B, First Lieutenant Harry F. Noyes, Jr., the range officer for Battery E, 3-inch Antiaircraft Group, 3d Defense Battalion, heard the sound of a loud explosion coming from the direction of the harbor at about 0750. First assuming that blasting crews were busy—there had been a lot of construction recently—Noyes cocked his ears. The new sounds seemed a bit different, "more higher-pitched, and louder." At that, he sprang from his bed, ran across the room, and peered northward just in time to see a dirty column of water rising from the harbor from another explosion and a Japanese plane pulling out of its dive. The plane, bearing red *hinomaru* (rising sun insignia) under its wings, left no doubt as to its identity.

*　　　*　　　*　　　*　　　*

The explosions likewise awakened Lieutenant Colonel William J. Whaling and Major James "Jerry" Monaghan who, while Colonel Gilder D. Jackson, commanding officer of the Marine Barracks, was at sea in *Indianapolis* (CA-35) en route to Johnston Island for tests of Higgins landing boats, shared his quarters at Pearl Harbor. Shortly before 0800, Whaling rolled over and asked: "Jerry, don't you think the Admiral is a little bit inconsiderate of guests?" Monaghan, then also awake, replied: "I'll go down and see about it." Whaling, meanwhile, lingered in bed until more blasts rattled the quarters' windows. Thinking that he had not seen any 5-inch guns emplaced close to the building, and that something was wrong, he got up and walked over to the window that faced the harbor. Looking out, he saw smoke, and, turning, remarked: "This thing is so real that I believe that's an oil tank burning right in front there." Both men then dressed and hurried across the parade ground, where they encountered Lieutenant Colonel Elmer E. Hall, commanding officer of the 2d Engineer Battalion. "Elmer," Whaling said amiably, "this is a mighty fine show you are putting on. I have never seen anything quite like it."

Department of Defense Photo (USMC) 65746

Col William J. Whaling, seen here circa 1945, was an observer to the Pearl Harbor attack, being awakened from slumber while staying in Col Gilder Jackson's quarters on the morning of 7 December.

Meanwhile, Swartz ordered the field music to sound "Call to Arms." Then, running into the officer's section of the mess hall, Swartz informed the officer-of-the-day, First Lieutenant Cornelius C. Smith, Jr., who had been enjoying a cup of coffee with Marine Gunner Floyd McCorkle when sharp blasts had rocked the building, that the Japanese were attacking. Like Swartz, they ran out onto the lanai. Standing there, speechless, they watched the first enemy planes diving on Ford Island.

Marines began to stumble, eyes wide in disbelief, from the barracks. Some were lurching, on the run, into pants and shirts; a few wore only towels. Swartz then ordered one of the platoon sergeants to roust out the men and get them under cover of the trees outside. Smith, too, then ran outside to the parade ground. As he looked at the rising smoke and the Japanese planes, he doubted those who had derided the "Japs" as "cross-eyed, second-rate pilots who couldn't hit the broad side of a barn door." It was enough to turn his stomach. "They're kicking the hell out of Pearl Harbor," he thought.

Meanwhile, unable to reach Colonel Harry B. Pickett, the 14th Naval District Marine Officer, as well as Colonel Jackson, and Captain Samuel R. Shaw, commanding officer of Company A, by telephone, Swartz sent runners to the officers' respective quarters. He then ordered a noncommissioned officer from the quartermaster department to dispense arms and ammunition.

While Swartz organized the men beneath the trees outside the barracks, Lieutenant Noyes dressed and then drove across the parade ground to Building 277, arriving about 0805. At the same time, like Swartz, First Lieutenant James S. O'Halloran, the 3d Defense Battalion's duty officer and commanding officer of Battery F, 3-inch Antiaircraft Group, wanted to get in touch with his senior officers. After having had "assembly" sounded and signalling his men to take cover, O'Halloran ordered Marine Gunner Frederick M. Steinhauser, the assistant battalion communications officer, to telephone all of the officers who resided outside the reservation and inform them of the attack.

In Honolulu, mustachioed Major Harold C. Roberts, acting commanding officer of the 3d Defense Battalion since Lieutenant Colonel Robert H. Pepper had accompanied Colonel Jackson to sea in *Indianapolis*, after taking Steinhauser's call with word of the bombing of Pearl, jumped into his car along with his neighbor, Major Kenneth W. Benner, commanding officer of the 3-inch Antiaircraft Group and the Headquarters and Service Battery of the 3d Defense Battalion. As Roberts' car crept through the heavy traffic toward Pearl, the two officers could see Japanese aircraft flying along the coast. When they reached the Water Street Fish Market, a large crowd of what seemed to be "Japanese residents ... cheering the Japanese planes, waving to them, and trying to obstruct traffic to Pearl Harbor by pushing parked cars into the street" blocked their way.

*   *   *   *   *

Meanwhile, as his acting battalion commander was battling his way through Honolulu's congested streets, O'Halloran was organizing his Marines as they poured out of the barracks into groups to break out small arms and machine guns from the various battalion storerooms. After Harry Noyes drove up, O'Halloran told him to do what he could to get the 3-inch guns, and fire control equipment, if available, broken out and set up, and then instructed other Marines to "get tractors and start hauling guns to the parade ground." Another detail of men hurried off to recover an antiaircraft director that lay crated and ready for shipment to Midway.

*   *   *   *   *

Marines continued to stream out onto the grounds, having been ordered out of the barracks with their rifles and cartridge belts; they doubled the sentry posts and received instructions to stand ready and armed, to deploy in an emergency. Noyes saw some Marines who had not been assigned any tasks commencing fire on enemy planes "which were considerably out of range." At the main gate of the Navy Yard, the Marines fired at whatever planes came close enough—sailors from the high-speed minelayer *Sicard* (DM-21), en route to their ship, later attested to seeing one Japanese plane shot down by the guards' rifle fire.

Tai Sing Loo, who was to have photographed those guards at the new gate, had left Honolulu in a hurry when he heard the sound of explosions and gunfire, and saw the rising columns of smoke. He arrived at the naval reservation without his Graflex and soon marveled at the cool bravery of the "young, fighting Marines" who stood their ground, under fire, blazing away at enemy planes with rifles while keeping traffic moving.

Finally, the more senior officers quartered outside the reservation began showing up. When Colonel Pickett arrived, Lieutenant Swartz returned to the officer-of-the-day's room and found that Captain Shaw had reached there also. Securing from his position as officer of the guard, Swartz returned to his 3-inch gun battery being set up near Building 277. Ordering Marines out of the building, he managed to obtain a steel helmet and a pistol each for himself and Lieutenant O'Halloran. Captain Samuel G. Taxis, commanding officer of the 3d Defense Battalion's 5-inch

- *45* -

Artillery Group, meanwhile, witnessed "terrific confusion" ensuing from his men's efforts to obtain "ammunition, steel helmets, and other items of equipment."

Smoke darkens the sky over the Marine Barracks complex at the Pearl Harbor Navy Yard; Marine in foreground appears to be holding his head in disbelief. Marines at far left in background appear to be unlimbering a 3-inch antiaircraft gun.

Meanwhile, the comparatively few Marines of Lieutenant Colonel Bert A. Bone's 1st Defense Battalion—most of which garrisoned Wake, Johnston, and Palmyra—made their presence felt. Urged on by Lieutenant Noyes, one detail of men immediately reported to the battalion gun shed and storerooms, and issued rifles and ammunition to all comers, while another detachment worked feverishly assembling machine guns. Navy Yard workmen—enginemen Lokana Kipihe and Oliver Bright, fireman Gerard Williams, and rigger Ernest W. Birch—appeared, looking for some way to help the Marines, who soon put them to work distributing ammunition to the machine gun crews. Soon, the Marines at the barracks added the staccato hammering of automatic weapons fire to the general din around them. Meanwhile, other Marines from the 1st Defense Battalion broke out firefighting equipment, as shrapnel from exploding antiaircraft shells began to strike the roof of the barracks and adjacent buildings.

At about 0820, Majors Roberts and Benner reached the Marine Barracks just in time to observe the beginning of the Japanese second wave attacks against Pearl. Roberts found that Lieutenant O'Halloran had gotten the 3d Battalion ready for battle, with seven .50-caliber and six .30-caliber machine guns set up and with ammunition belted. Under Captain Harry O. Smith, Jr., commanding officer of Battery H, Machine Gun Group, 3d Defense Battalion, the 3d's Marine gunners had already claimed one Japanese plane shot down. Lieutenant Noyes was, meanwhile, in the process of deploying seven 3-inch guns—three on the west end of the parade ground and four on the east.

Sergeant Major Leland H. Alexander, of the Headquarters and Service Battery of the 3d Defense Battalion, suggested to Lieutenant O'Halloran that an armed convoy be organized to secure ammunition for the guns, as none was available in the Navy Yard proper. Roberts gave Alexander permission to put together the requisite trucks, weapons, and men. Lieutenant Colonel Bone had the same idea, and, accordingly dispatched a truck at 0830 to the nearest ammunition dump near Fort Kamehameha. Bone ordered another group of men from the 5-inch battery to the Naval Ammunition Depot at Lualualei just in case. He hoped that at least one truck would get through the maelstrom of traffic. Marines from the 2d Engineer Battalion made ammunition runs as well as provided men and motorcycles for messengers.

Meanwhile, Roberts directed Major Benner to have the 3d Battalion's guns operational before the ammunition trucks returned, and to set the fuzes for 1,000 yards, since the guns lacked the necessary height-finding equipment. The makeshift emplacements, however, presented less than ideal firing positions since the barracks and nearby yard buildings restricted the field of fire, and many of the low-flying planes appeared on the horizon only for an instant.

Necessity often being the mother of invention, Roberts devised an impromptu fire control system, stationing a warning section of eight men, equipped with field glasses and led by Lieutenant Swartz, in the center of the parade ground. The spotters were to pass the word to a group of field musics who, using their instruments, were to sound appropriate warnings: one blast meant planes approaching from the north; two blasts, from the east, and so on.

Taking precautions against fires in the temporary wooden barracks, Roberts ordered hoses run out and extinguishers placed in front of them, along with shovels, axes, and buckets of sand (the latter to deal with incendiary bombs); hose reel and chemical carts placed near the center hydrant near the mess hall; and all possible containers filled with water for both fighting fires and drinking. In addition, he ordered cooks and messmen to prepare coffee and fill every other container on hand with water, and organized riflemen in groups of about 16 to sit on the ground with an officer or noncommissioned officer in charge to direct their fire. He also called for runners from all groups in the battalion and established his command post at the parade ground's south corner, and ordered the almost 150 civilians who had showed up looking for ways to help out to report to the machine gun storeroom and fill ammunition belts and clean weapons. Among other actions, he also instructed the battalion sergeant major to be ready to safeguard important papers from the headquarters barracks.

*   *   *   *   *

Prior to Roberts' arrival, Lieutenant (j.g.) William R. Franklin (Dental Corps), USN, the dental officer for the 3d Defense Battalion's Headquarters and Service Battery, and the only medical officer present, had organized first aid and stretcher parties in the barracks. As the other doctors arrived, Roberts directed them to set up dressing stations at each battalion headquarters and one at sick bay. Elsewhere, Marines vacated one 100-man temporary barracks, the noncommissioned officer's club and the post exchange, to ready them for casualties. Parties of Marines also reported to the waterfront area to assist in collecting and transporting casualties from the ships in the harbor to the Naval Hospital.

By the time the Marines had gotten their new fire precautions in place, the Japanese second wave attack was in full swing. Although their pilots selected targets exclusively from among the Pacific Fleet warships, the Marines at the barracks in the Navy Yard still were able to take the Japanese planes, most of which seemed to be coming in from the west and southwest, under fire. While Marines were busily setting up the 3-inch guns, several civilian yard workmen grabbed up rifles and "brought their fire to bear upon the enemy," allowing Swartz's men to continue their work.

Oily smoke from the burning Arizona *(BB-39) boils up in the background beyond the Navy Yard water towers, one of them, in center, signal-flag bedecked. Note several Marines attempting to deploy a 3-inch antiaircraft gun in the foreground.*

The Japanese eventually put Major Roberts' ingenious fire control methods—the field musics—to the test. After hearing four hearty blasts from the bandsmen, the .50-calibers began hammering out cones of tracer that caught two low-flying dive bombers as they pulled out of their runs over Pearl, prompting Roberts' fear that the ships would fire at them, too, and hit the barracks. One Val slanted earthward near what appeared to be either the west end of the lower tank farm or the south end of the Naval Hospital reservation, while the other, emitting great quantities of smoke, crashed west-southwest of the parade ground.

Although the Marines success against their tormentors must have seemed sweet indeed, a skeptical Captain Taxis thought it more likely that the crews of the two Vals bagged by the machine gunners had just run out of luck. Most of the firing, in his opinion, had been quite ineffectual, mostly "directed at enemy planes far beyond range of the weapons and merely fired into the air at no target at all." Gunners on board the fleet's warships were faring little better!

Almost simultaneously with the dive-bombing attacks, horizontal bombing attacks began. Major Roberts noted that the 18 bombers "flew in two Vees of nine planes each in column of Vees and [that] they kept a good formation." At least some of those planes appeared to have bombed the battleship *Pennsylvania* and the destroyers *Cassin* and *Downes* in Dry Dock No. 1. In the confusion, however, Roberts probably saw two divisions of *Kates* from *Zuikaku* preparing for their attack runs on Hickam Field. A single division of such planes from *Shokaku*, meanwhile, attacked the Navy Yard and the Naval Air Station.

Well removed from the barracks, Marines assigned to the Navy Yards Fire Department rendered invaluable assistance in leading critical firefighting efforts. Heading the department, Sergeant Harold F. Abbott supervised the distribution of the various units, and coordinated the flood of volunteers who stepped forward to help.

One of Abbott's men, Private First Class Marion M. Milbrandt, with his 1,000-gallon pumper, summoned to the Naval Hospital grounds, found that one of *Kaga*'s Kates—struck by machine gun fire from the ships moored in the Repair Basin—had crashed near there. The resulting fire, fed by the crashed plane's gasoline, threatened the facility, but Milbrandt and his crew controlled the blaze.

Other Marine firefighters were hard at work alongside Dry Dock No. 1. *Pennsylvania* had not been the only ship not fully ready for war, since she lay immobile at one end of the drydock. *Downes* lay in the dock, undergoing various items of work, while *Cassin* had been having ordnance alterations at the Yard and thus had none of her 5-inch/38s ready for firing. Both destroyers soon came in for some unwanted attention.

As bombs turned the two destroyers into cauldrons of flames and their crews abandoned ship, two sailors from *Downes*, meanwhile, sprinted over to the Marine Barracks: Gunner's Mate First Class Michael G. Odietus and Gunner's Mate Second Class Curtis P. Schulze. After the order to abandon ship had been given, both had, on their own initiative, gone to the Marine Barracks to assist in the distribution of arms and ammunition. They soon returned, however, each gunner's mate with a Browning Automatic Rifle in hand, to do his part in fighting back.

Antiaircraft Gun Fired to a Range of 14,500 Yards

A 5-inch/25-caliber open pedestal mount antiaircraft gun—manned here by sailors on board the heavy cruiser *Astoria* (CA-34) in early 1942—was the standard battleship and heavy cruiser antiaircraft weapon at Pearl Harbor. The mount itself weighed more than 20,000 pounds, while the gun fired a 53.8-pound projectile to a maximum range (at 45 degrees elevation) of 14,500 yards. It was a weapon such as this that Sergeants Hailey and Wears, and Private First Class Curran, after the sinking of their ship, *Oklahoma* (BB-37), helped man on board *Maryland* (BB-46) on 7 December 1941.

Utilizing three of the department's pumpers, meanwhile, the first firefighters from the yard, who included Corporal John Gimson, Privates First Class William M. Brashear, William A. Hopper, Peter Kerdikes, Frank W. Feret, Marvin D. Dallman, and Corporal Milbrandt, among them, soon arrived and began to play water on the burning ships. At about 0915, four torpedo warheads on board *Downes* cooked off and exploded, the concussion tearing the hoses from the hands of the men fighting the blaze and sending fragments everywhere, temporarily forcing all hands to retreat to the nearby road and sprawl there. Knocked flat several times by the explosions, the Marines and other firefighters, which included men from *Cassin* and *Downes*, and civilian yard workmen, remained on the job.

Explosions continued to wrack the two destroyers, while subsequent partial flooding of the dock caused *Cassin* to pivot on her forefoot and heel over onto her sister ship. Working under the direction of Lieutenant William R. Spear, a 57-year-old retired naval officer called to the colors, the firemen were understandably concerned that the oil fires burning in proximity to the two destroyers might drift aft in the partially flooded dry dock and breach the caisson, unleashing a wall of water that would carry *Pennsylvania* (three of whose four propeller shafts had been pulled for overhaul) down upon the burning destroyers. Preparing for that eventuality, Private First-Class Don O. Femmer, in charge of the 750-gallon pumper, stood ready should the conflagration spread to the northeast through the dock.

Fortunately, circumstances never required Femmer and his men to defend the caisson from fire, but the young private had more than his share of troubles, when his pumper broke down at what could have been a critical moment. Undaunted, Femmer made temporary repairs and stood his ground at the caisson throughout the raid.

At the opposite end of the dry dock, meanwhile, Private First-Class Omar E. Hill fared little better with his 500-gallon pumper. As if the firefighting labors were not arduous enough, a ruptured circulating water line threatened to shut down his fire engine. Holding a rag on the broken line while his comrades raced away to obtain spare parts, Hill kept his pumper in the battle.

National Archives Photo 80-G-32739

While firefighters train massive jets of water from dockside at left,
Shaw *(DD-373) burns in the Floating Drydock YFD-2, after being
hit by three bombs. Tug* Sotoyomo *(YT-9), with which* Shaw *has
been sharing the drydock, is barely visible ahead of the crippled
destroyer. Marines led these firefighting efforts on 7 December
1941.*

Meanwhile, firefighters on the west side of the dock succeeded in passing
three hoses to men on *Pennsylvania*'s forecastle, where they directed blasts
of water ahead of the ship and down the starboard side to prevent the burning
oil, which resembled a "seething cauldron," from drifting aft. A second 500-
gallon engine crew, led by Private First Class Dallman, battled the fires at
the southwest end of the drydock, despite the suffocating oily black smoke
billowing forth from *Cassin* and *Downes*. Eventually, by 1035, the Marines
and other volunteers—who included the indomitable Tai Sing Loo—had
succeeded in quelling the fires on board *Cassin*; those on board *Downes* were
put out early that afternoon.

More work, however, lay in store for Corporal Milbrandt and his crew.
Between 0755 and 0900, three Vals had attacked the destroyer *Shaw* (DD-
373), which shared *YFD-2* with the little yard tug *Sotoyomo*. All three scored
hits. Fires ultimately reached *Shaw*'s forward magazines and triggered an
explosion that sent tendrils of smoke into the sky and severed the ship's bow.
Several other volunteer units were already battling the blaze with hose carts
and two 350-gallon pumpers sent in from Honolulu. Milbrandt, aided as well
by the Pan American Airways fire boat normally stationed at Pearl City,
ultimately succeeded in extinguishing the stricken destroyer's fires.

In the meantime, after having pounded the military installations on Oahu for nearly two hours, between 0940 and 1000 the Japanese planes made their way westward to return to the carrier decks from whence they had arisen. With the respite offered by the enemy's departure (no one knew for sure whether or not they would be back), the Marines at last found time to take stock of their situation. Fortunately, the Marine Barracks lay some distance away from what had interested the Japanese the most: the ships in the harbor proper. Although some "shell fragments literally rained at times" the material loss sustained by the barracks was slight. Moreover, it had been American gunfire from the ships in the harbor, rather than bombs from Japanese planes overhead, that had inflicted the damage; at one point that morning a 3-inch antiaircraft shell crashed through the roof of a storehouse—the only damage sustained by the barracks during the entire attack.

Considering the carnage at the airfields on Oahu, and especially, among the units of the Pacific Fleet, only four men of the 3d Defense Battalion had been wounded: Sergeant Samuel H. Cobb, Jr., of the 3d Defense Battalion's 3-inch Antiaircraft Group, suffered head injuries serious enough to warrant his being transferred to the Naval Hospital for treatment, while Private First Class Jules B. Maioran and Private William J. Whitcomb of the Machine Gun Group and Sergeant Leo Hendricks II, of the Headquarters and Service Battery, suffered less serious injuries. In addition, two men sent with the trucks to find ammunition for the 3-inch batteries suffered injuries when they fell off the vehicles.

In their subsequent reports, the defense battalion and barracks officers declined to single out individuals, noting no outstanding individual behavior during the raid—only the steady discharge of duty expected of Marines. To be sure, great confusion existed, especially at first, but the command quickly settled down to work and "showed no more than the normal excitement and no trace of panic or even uneasiness." If anything, the Marines tended to place themselves at risk unnecessarily, as they went about their business coolly and, in many cases, "in utter disregard of their own safety." Major Roberts recommended that the entire 3d Defense Battalion be commended for "their initiative, coolness under fire, and [the] alacrity with which they emplaced their guns."

Commendations, however, were not the order of the day on 7 December. Although the Japanese had left, the Marines expected them to return and finish the job they had begun (many Japanese pilots, including Fuchida, wanted to do just that). If another attack was to come, there was much to do to prepare for it. As the skies cleared of enemy planes, the Marines at the barracks secured their establishment and took steps to complete the work already begun on the defenses. At 1030, the 3d Defense Battalion's corporal of the guard moved to the barracks and set the battalion's radio to the Army Information Service frequency, thus enabling them to pass "flash" messages to all groups. The Marines also distributed gas masks to all hands.

The morning and afternoon passed quickly, the men losing track of time. The initial confusion experienced during the opening moments of the raid had by that point given way to at least some semblance of order, as officers and noncoms arrived from leave and began to sort out their commands. At 1105, the 3d Defense Battalion's Battery G deployed to makeshift defense positions as an infantry reserve in some ditches dug for building foundations. All of the messmen, many of whom had taken an active hand in the defense of the barracks against the Japanese attack, returned to the three general mess halls and opened up an around-the-clock service to all comers, including "about 6,000 meals ... to the civilian workmen of the navy yard," a service discontinued only "after the food supply at the regular established eating places could be replenished."

By 1100, at least some of the 3-inch batteries were emplaced and ready to answer any future Japanese raids. At the north end of the parade ground, the 3d Defense Battalion's Battery D stood ready for action at 1135 while another battery, consisting of three guns and an antiaircraft director (the one originally earmarked for Midway) lay at the south end. At 1220, Major Roberts organized his battalion's strength into six task groups. Task group no. 1 was to double the Navy Yard guard force, no. 2 was to provide antiaircraft defense, and no. 3 was to provide machine gun defense. No. 4 was to provide infantry reserve and firefighting crews, no. 5 was to coordinate transportation, and no. 6 was to provide ammunition and equipment, as well as messing and billeting support.

National Archives Photo 80-G-19943

In the aftermath of the attack, Pennsylvania *(BB-38) lies astern of the wrecked destroyers* Cassin *(DD-372) and* Downes *(DD-375) in Dry Dock No. 1. Light cruiser* Helena *(CL-50) lies alongside 1010 Dock in right background; pall of smoke is from the still-burning* Arizona *(BB-39). Marine firefighters distinguished themselves in battling blazes in this area.*

By 1300, meanwhile, all of the fires in Dry Dock No. 1 had been extinguished, permitting the Marine and civilian firefighters to secure their hard-worked equipment. Although the two battered destroyers, *Cassin* and *Downes*, appeared to be total losses, those who had battled the blaze could take great satisfaction in knowing that they had not only spared *Pennsylvania* from serious fire damage but had also played a major role in saving the drydock. As Tai Sing Loo recounted later in his own brand of English: "The Marines of the Fire Dep[artmen]t of the Navy Yard are the Heroes of the Day of Dec. 7, 1941 that save the *Cassin* and *Downes* and USS *Pennsylvania* in Dry Dock No. 1."

Later that afternoon, Battery D's four officers and 68 enlisted men, with four .30-caliber machine guns sent along with them for good measure, moved from the barracks over to Hickam Field to provide the Army installation some measure of antiaircraft protection. Hickam also benefitted from the provision of the 2d Engineer Battalion's service and equipment. After the attack, the battalion's dump truck and two bulldozers lumbered over to the stricken air base to assist in clearing what remained of the bombers that had been parked wingtip to wingtip, and filling bomb craters.

*   *   *   *   *

Around 1530, a Marine patrol approached Tai Sing Loo, a familiar figure about the Navy Yard, and asked him to do them a favor. They had had no lunch; some had had no breakfast because of the events of the day. Going to the garage, Loo rode his bright red "putput" over to the 3d Defense Battalion mess hall and related to his old friend Technical Sergeant Joseph A. Newland the tale of the hungry Marines. Newland and his messmen prepared ham and chicken sandwiches and Loo made the rounds of all the posts he could reach.

*   *   *   *   *

In the afternoon and early evening hours of 7 December, the men received reports that their drinking water was poisoned, and that various points on Oahu were being bombed and/or invaded. In the absence of any real news, such alarming reports—especially when added to the already nervous state of the defenders—only fueled the fear and paranoia prevalent among all ranks and rates. In addition, most of the men were exhausted after their exertions of the morning and afternoon. Dog-tired, many would remain on duty for 36 hours without relief. Drawn, unshaven faces and puffy eyes were common. Tense, expectant and anxious Marines and sailors at Pearl spent a fitful night on the 7th.

It is little wonder that mistakes would be made that would have tragic consequences, especially in the stygian darkness of that first blacked-out Hawaiian night following the raid. Still some hours away from Oahu, the carrier *Enterprise* and her air group had been flying searches and patrols throughout the day, in a so-far fruitless effort to locate the Japanese carrier force. South of Oahu, one of her pilots spotted what he thought was a Japanese ship and *Enterprise* launched a 31-plane strike at 1642. Nagumo's fleet, however, was homeward bound. While *Enterprise* recovered the torpedo planes and dive bombers after their fruitless search, she directed the fighters to land at NAS Pearl Harbor.

Machine guns on board the battleship *Pennsylvania* opened fire on the flight as it came for a landing, though, and soon the entire harbor exploded into a fury of gunfire as cones of tracers converged on the incoming "Wildcats." Three of the F4Fs slanted earthward almost immediately; a fourth crashed a short time later. Two managed to land at Ford Island. The 3d Defense Battalion's journalist later recorded that "six planes with running lights under 400 feet altitude tried Ford Island landing and were machine gunned." It was a tragic footnote to what had been a terrible day indeed.

The Marines at Pearl Harbor had been surprised by the attack that descended upon them, but they rose to the occasion and fought back in the "best traditions of the naval service." While the enemy had attacked with tenacity and daring, no less so was the response from the Marines on board the battleships and cruisers, at Ewa Mooring Mast Field, and at the Marine Barracks. One can only think that Admiral Isoroku Yamamoto's worst fears of America's "terrible resolve" and that he had awakened a sleeping giant would have been confirmed if he could have peered into the faces, so deeply etched with grim determination, of the Marines who had survived the events of that December day in 1941.

Photo courtesy of Mrs. Evelyn Lee, via Paul Stillwell,
U.S. Naval Institute

Tai Sing Loo and His Bright Red 'Putput'

Tai Sing Loo, Navy Yard photographer, had scheduled an appointment to take a picture of the Main Gate guards at the Navy Yard on the morning of 7 December 1941. While he ended up not taking pictures of the Marines, he gallantly helped the Marines of the Navy Yard Fire Department put out fires in Dry Dock No. 1 and later delivered food to famished Leathernecks. He is seen here on his famous bright red "putput" that he drove around the yard that day delivering sandwiches and fruit juice.

Pearl Harbor Remembered

Several of the many memoirs in the Marine Corps Oral History Collection are by Marines who were serving at Pearl Harbor on 7 December 1941, and personally witnessed the Japanese attack. Two such memoirs—one by Lieutenant General Alan Shapley and a second by Brigadier General Samuel R. Shaw—vividly describe the events of that day as they remembered it. General Shapley, a major in December 1941, had been relieved as commander of *Arizona*'s Marine detachment on the 6th. He recalled:

I was just finishing my breakfast, and I was just about ready to go to my room and get in my baseball uniform to play the *Enterprise* for the baseball championship of the United States Fleet, and I heard this terrible bang and crash. I thought it was a motor sailer that they dropped on the fantail, and I ran up there to see what it was all about. When I got up on deck there, the sailors were aligned on the railing there, looking towards Pearl Harbor, and I heard two or three of them say, 'This is the best damned drill the Army Air Corps has ever put on.' Then we saw a destroyer being blown up in the dry dock across the way.

The first thing I knew was when the fantail, which was wood, was being splintered when we were being strafed by machine guns. And then there was a little bit of confusion, and I can remember this because they passed the word on ship that all unengaged personnel get below the third deck. You see, in a battleship the third deck is the armored deck, and so realizing what was going on, this attack and being strafed, the unengaged personnel were ordered below the third deck.

That started some people going down the ladders. Then right after that, the *Pennsylvania*, which was the flagship of the whole fleet, put up these signals, "Go to general quarters." So that meant that the people were going the other way too. Lt [Carleton E.] Simensen did quite a job of turning some of the sailors around, and we went up in the director. [On the way up the mainmast tripod, Lt Simensen was killed.] He caught a burst through the heart and almost knocked me off the tripod because I was behind him on the ladder, and I boosted him up in the searchlight platform and went in to my director. And of course, when I got up there, there were only seven or eight men there, and I thought we were all going to get cooked to death because I couldn't see anything but fire below after a while. I stayed there and watched this whole attack, because I had a grandstand seat for that, and then it got pretty hot. Anyway, the wind was blowing from the stern to the stem and I sent the men down and got those men off. Then I apparently got knocked off or blown off.

I was pretty close to shore.... There was a dredging pipeline that ran between the ship and Ford Island. And I guess that I was only about 25 yards from the pipeline and 10 yards from Ford Island, and managed to get ashore. I wasn't so much covered with oil. I didn't have any clothes on. [The burning fuel oil] burnt all my clothes off. I walked up to the airfield which wasn't very bright of me, because this was still being attacked at first. I wanted to get a machine gun in the administration building but I couldn't do that. Then I was given a boat cloak from one of my men. It was quite a sight to see 400 or 500 men walking around all burnt, just like charred steak. You could just see their eyes and their mouths. It was terrible. Later I went over to the island and went to the Marine barracks and got some clothes.

At the Marine Barracks, Captain Samuel R. Shaw, who commanded one of the two barracks companies, vividly remembered that Sunday morning as well:

The boat guards were in place, and the music was out there, and the old and new officer of the day. And we had a music, and a hell of a fine sergeant bugler who had been in Shanghai. He would stand beside the officers of the day, and there came the airplanes, and he looked up and he said, "Captain, those are Japanese war planes." And one of the two of them said, "My God, they are, sound the call to arms." So the bugler started sounding the call to arms before the first bomb hit.

Of course they had already started taking out the machine guns. They didn't wait for the key in the OD's office, they just broke the door down and hauled out the machine guns, put them in position. Everybody that wasn't involved in that drill grabbed their rifles and ran out in the parade ground, and starting firing at the airplanes. They must have had several hundred men out there with rifles. And every [Japanese] plane that was recovered there, or pieces of it, had lots of .30-caliber holes—somebody was hitting them, machine guns or rifles.

Then I remembered—here we had all these guys on the post who had not been relieved, and they had been posted at 4 o'clock, and come 9 o'clock, 9:30 they not only had not been relieved but had no chow and no water. So I got hold of the mess sergeant and told him to organize, to go around to the posts.

They had a depot. At the beginning it was a supply depot. I told him to send a party over there and draw a lot of canteens and make sandwiches, and we'd send water and sandwiches around to the guys on posts until we found out some way to relieve all these guys, and get people back. Then he told me that it was fine except that he didn't have nearly enough messmen, they were all out in the parade ground shooting. I think the second phase of planes came in at that time and we had a hell of an uproar.

Sources

The authors consulted primary materials in the Marine Corps Historical
Center Reference Section (November/December 1941 muster rolls) and
Personal Papers Section (Claude A. Larkins, Roger M. Emmons, and
Wayne Jordan collections), as well as in the Naval Historical Center
Operational Archives Branch (action reports and/or microfilmed deck
logs for the 15 ships with embarked Marine Detachments, and those units
included in the Commandant, 14th Naval District, report), in the office
of the Coast Guard Historian, and in the Gordon W. Prange Papers.

The *Pearl Harbor Attack: Hearings Before the Joint Committee on the
Investigation of the Pearl Harbor Attack* (Washington, D.C.:
Government Printing Office, 1946) contains useful accounts (Lieutenant
Commander Fuqua, Lieutenant Colonel Whaling, and Lieutenant
Colonel Larkin), as does Paul Stillwell, ed., *Air Raid: Pearl Harbor!
Recollections of a Day of Infamy* (Annapolis: Naval Institute Press,
1981).

General works concerning Pearl Harbor that were consulted include
Gordon W. Prange, et al., *December 7, 1941: The Day The Japanese
Attacked Pearl Harbor* (New York: McGraw Hill, 1987), Walter Lord,
Day of Infamy (Henry Holt & Co., 1957), and Japanese War History
Office, *Senshi Sosho* [War History Series], Vol. 10, *Hawaii Sakusen*
(Tokyo: Asagumo Shimbunsa, 1970).

Articles from the *Naval Institute Proceedings* include: Cornelius C.
Smith Jr., "... A Hell of a Christmas," (Dec68), Thomas C. Hone, "The
Destruction of the Battle Line at Pearl Harbor," (Dec77) and Paul H.
Backus, "Why Them And Not Me?" (Sep81). From *Marine Corps
Gazette*: Clifford B. Drake, "A Day at Pearl Harbor," (Nov65). From
Shipmate: Samuel R. Shaw, "Marine Barracks, Navy Yard, Pearl
Harbor," (Dec73). From *Naval History*: Albert A. Grasselli, "The Ewa
Marines" (Spring 1991). From *Leatherneck*: Philip N. Pierce, "Twenty
Years Ago ..." (Dec61)

About the Authors

Robert J. Cressman is currently a civilian historian in the Naval Historical Center's Ships' Histories Branch. A graduate of the University of Maryland with a bachelor of arts in history in 1972, he obtained his master of arts in history under the late Dr. Gordon W. Prange at the University of Maryland in 1978. Mr.  Cressman, a former reference historian in the Marine Corps Historical Center's Reference Section (1979–1981), is author of *That Gallant Ship: USS Yorktown (CV-5)*, and editor and principal contributor of *A Glorious Page in Our History: The Battle of Midway, 4–6 June 1942*. He and the co-author of this monograph, J. Michael Wenger, also co-authored *Steady Nerves and Stout Hearts: The USS Enterprise (CV-6) Air Group and Pearl Harbor, 7 December 1941*.

J. Michael Wenger, currently an analyst for the Square D Company in Knightdale, North Carolina, graduated from Atlantic Christian College in 1972, and  obtained a master of arts from Duke University in 1973. Mr. Wenger has taught in the Raleigh, North Carolina, school system and writes as a free-lance military historian. He is the co-author of *The Way It Was: Pearl Harbor—The Original Photographs*. His publication credits include the Raleigh *News and Observer* and *Naval Aviation News*.